Love Letters to BALLED FISTS

EBONY STEWART

Stewart, Ebony
1st edition.
ISBN: 978-0-989-00920-1

Edited by Mike Whalen, Kevin Burke, and C.B. Renz
Proofread by Jacob Dodson
Cover and Interior layout design by Amy McDonnold

Printed in Tennessee, USA

Timber Mouse Publishing
Austin, TX
www.timbermouse.com

To contact the author, please email ebpoetry@gmail.com

TABLE OF CONTENTS

"You have to be willing to be happy about nothing."
~Andy Warhol

MOSAIC WOMEN

I come from a long line of story tellers.
Not the kind of story tellers that lie.
But the kind that make believe for a living.
The kind who sit up straight,
could give a damn about David or Goliath,
and words like the axe Jack used for the beanstalk.
The kind whose bellies swell and shake when they talk.
Whose throats grind and minds engineer.

Women raised me.

Women who can smother anything and swallow feelings whole.
Round women,
whose booties used to be table tops,
now they fold for alter prayer.
Their mother taught us how.
Sway women.
Love, lose and gather women.

Women, whose hair doesn't match their skin.
You'd have to be "pretty for a dark skin girl" to know what I mean.

The kind that carry bundles and bags wear a doo rag and cuss.
Closed fist women.
Open arms and legs too wide women.
Single household women.
My mother say her kids'll never want for nothin'.
Got one auntie say, "If you ain't speakin' guapanese, you can't be
talkin' to me!"

These women,
who carry a pen, a switchblade, and bubble gum in their purses.
I say these women, make the world go 'round in verses.

BACKWARDS DRIVING

I'm not sure what type of girl I am
or the kind of woman I think I still have time to be.
Everything about my life reminds me of blowing bubbles.
Things take effort, look pretty and simple up in the air
falling all over the sky,
floating like foxtails with eyes like iridescent goldfish.
Everything has promise and then
    pop!
We're all grassroots going up.

Does anyone else make wishes with their fallen eyelashes?
I know I do.

I am always a little bit odd
and out sitting inside my backpack
or the ghost streak side of an eraser.
Most times I do this to myself.
I want to be so New York,
but not even Texas will let me go.
I've decided that means I'm worth keeping,
but I'm such a small thing in Texas.

I've decided that every time the clock picks 11:22,
   it's my birthday!
I've been born twice a day for 30 years and it's not getting
   any easier.
I wish I knew what kind of people my parents were before
   they met me.
I feel the need to hide things about myself.
The day I cut imaginary eyelids into my wrists and realized the
   slits were too deep, I knew I was human

that I knew how to die

and started wearing bracelets and hairbows 'round my wrists.
It's not all depressing.
I'm sure my smile has saved someone's life before.

I try daily, in mirrors.
I find my cookie crumbs and curiosity, even ears,
    dangling from my fingernails like everybody else.
I love to tell stories and make laughter through stampede chests
    or see the earth turn to green after the storm.
Red birds catch my attention;
sunrays making peek-a-boo skies do too.
I am not a fan of blue bonnets, but I like how they choose where
    to spread themselves.
I am not picky, but selective.
I also believe that sharing is an option,
not an obligation.
It can be dangerous to give too much of yourself,
but maybe if someone would've taught me how to love right,
I'd be able to keep things in my hands longer and not
    write so plain.

People love to read things they don't understand.
I love quotes and Chinese proverbs.
Oh! And cupcakes.

I take my time describing other people,
but treat Ebony like a cheap card trick in Vegas.
People only want to see the lights,
not meet the man who made them,
and we're all a burning cigarette bud.
Holding a drag is one of the most delicate things a gangster
    can do.
Peacing brown rolled up confetti between two insect tentacles.
Rubbing the others together like a praying mantis.
I don't want to be smoke or tipped leavings.

Is it weird to want to be a disease you'll never get rid of,
so even if you don't want me there, you can't help but
    deal with me?
Sometimes I make up things that sound like the truth.
I just need to be loved.
It all hurts.

At night, while lying in bed,
if I close my eyes quick enough, I can play a reel of my mother.
I've got too many poems about her and I don't care.
Since when are there too many stars in the sky?
She loves me more than I pay attention to how or why.
What will happen when her leaves fall and branches dry?
I imagine I'll be a mess of emotions and revolving doors.
Shrinking.
The last thing I'll need is to be in an empty room
of thoughts and things I cannot change.

I should totally stop forgetting how blessed I am.

Things my mother never taught me:
   1: If a girl goes without panties is it still called "going
      commando"?
   2: How do you make love to the Hulk?
I mean, without Bruce Banner showing up with all his deflated
   self trying to calm us down.
I am more like Rihanna finding love in a hopeless place than I
   care to admit.
Finding love that doesn't suit me seems to be an unhealthy
   formula of mine.
Hotel or not, I still make the pillows hold me like they're human.
I love both genders evenly, which means sometimes not at all.

Does anyone else like to watch dogs while they sleep?
I know I do.

I have the weight of my mother's gaze and short highway legs
   with not enough options.
I often confuse adaptation with intention.
By the end of this,
I plan to have it all figured out
and the rest is just a cry for help.

"Don't ever discount your tears. They can be healing
waters and a stream of joy. Sometimes they are
the best words the heart can't speak." ~ William P. Young

"Being alive and being a woman and being colored is a metaphysical dilemma I haven't conquered yet."

~ Ntozake Shange

TOMBOY

Mama say,
"Don't get wrapped up day dreamin''bout some boy
'specially when he wouldn't eva look yo way.
You could have 'em if you wanted too, you'd just have to do
    too much to get 'em."

That 'on't make 'em act right, though.
And I on't know how to make hot water cornbread.
I just like to eat it.
Every time I walk by Mr. Nussaum house, while he sittin' on
    his porch, he say
"Gu, what chu good fah?"
I tell him, none of his gotdamn businesss, under my breath.
Sometimes I wish his old ass could hear me.

Mama always sayin' I gotta know when to speak soft; don't lose
    my head just 'cause.

Mrs. Neil say,
"She got mo' pants than she got dresses, gone forget she a girl."
But the world ain't gone ever let me forget what's between
    my legs.
I be wantin' to say something to her too
but she press our hair
so mama say keep ya head straight so I won't get burned.
But Mrs. Neil'll burn you anyway.

"All this hair! Bet not be tender headed!"
Tender headed ain't got nothing to do with you burnin' me.
I always wonder when she gone die,
but then who gone do our hair?

Wearin' pants don't make you a boy.
And they don't hear you right when you got on a dress.
Just make you less in they mind.
Last time I wore a dress, I caught Johnny Hart tryin' to look up it.
What I do?

I chased him down the street with a butcher knife, see how many
    coochies he wanna look at after that!

So many names for it.
Pee-Pee.
Who-Who.
Poon-nana.
Boys act stupid once they figure out chu got one.
The Jamaican and Creole side of me call it a coochie or a twat.
Whatever you wanna call it, Johnny Hart wasn't gone see mine!

Yeah, I like boys okay, I guess.
Read this one book, author Mahogany L. Browne say,
"Boys are dumb, throw rocks at 'em."
I be throwin' rocks at this one boy all the time.
He only like girls who wear dresses and hair bows,
and don't throw rocks.
I caught him lookin', at me one time.
But he stopped.
Probably cause I told 'em I'd give him a knuckle sandwich if he
    kept staring at me.
So, he stopped.
Now every time I want him to look at me, he ain't.
He must don't know I got one.
A coochie, I mean.
Not a knuckle sandwich.

Mama say some men don't know what they want,
so how we expect a boy to?
I say, if he do like girls who wear dresses, he'll never look my way,
and the only thing he'll ever see in my hair is a pencil.
I heard Mrs. Porter say after church one day,
"Don't no man want no woman who always thinkin', readin', and
    writin' all the time."
They say me writing poetry is a dead giveaway.
But mama say I'm talented
and hers
and that's all that matters.
And if they were really reading the bible they'd know how that

one scripture go,
"He who finds a woman finds a good thing."
Or something like that.
It don't say nothing 'bout what she wearin', that she readin',
writin', or thinkin'.

MENARCHE

The first time my insides were painted red
I hid in white walls with matching toilets.
My breasts were tender and growing larger than my hands.
They were no longer fists.

My voice shrunk of power.
Anger, for no explained reason, lived in my eyebrows.
I kept tears on my eyelashes,
and maxi pads in the front zipper of my backpack.

With a house full of women, my mothers never treated
    menarche as a curse.
They did not punish me or hide me in black fabric or pretend
    not to know.
They said there'd be blessings that looked like red spots
    in my panties.
I wasn't sick.
I could still play sports.
I was what happened when spoken word and rap got together.
I tasted sweeter now.

A woman.

They called me special.
I'd be full and beside myself
and would figure out how to keep my hands on my hips.
Instead of slapping my face,
my mama would forgive me silver
and still think of me as gold.

Mothers have to use a different cupid with their daughters than
    they would with their sons.

The first time a boy noticed me, we fell in love on accident.
We called each other "boyfriend" and "girlfriend."
My friends knew we were "going out."
He held my hand and my books.

We both held the phone for hours with nothing received on the end.
He never touched my strawberry.
I think he loves me still.

The second time a boy noticed me, he sniffed me out and did not
    hear me say, "No."
He cupped my wrists of movement.
Someone has shown him how to love wrong.
He didn't care if it hurt or if his breath sounded like white noise
    against my neck.

Mute.

We are mute now.

Finding volume in our thoughts or poetry that Jamaica Kincaid
    writes.

When quiet
I am standing outside in Chicago, a blizzard, a snowstorm.
On days when I am a high-beamed woman, I stand in Queens.
I slow down subways and change into traffic lights.
I am dangerous like the upper and lower split on I-35.

When a girl becomes a woman and
she is peculiar,
leaking,
swelling,
raging hormones, and
lived-in jeans where she keeps her jewels,
make her pure.
Boys have a way of making girls rusty.
Tell her ivory is acceptable and linen is supposed to be wrinkled.
Treat her equal.
In life, she will take care of more than babydolls and
    Easy-Bake Ovens.
Girls can be cruel and boys learn how to speak in double
    standards.
She will wake up some days not enough for the Sun.

Her best friend and arch-enemy will always be herself,
a two-way glass mirror.

Her seasons will change more times than she's able to get
  used to,
but beauty still knows all of her by name.

DOMESTIC

For the boy on the basketball court who started a fight with my
   ex-boyfriend
and told him he hits like a girl,
to prove you wrong
he now hits girls too.

To his dad, who taught him how to kiss the girls and make
   them cry,
not only does he have your smile,
he also has your fist of rage
and unapologetic regrets.
Oh yeah,
and his left is just as strong as his right.
To his mother, who said, "sometimes women need to know when
   they are getting out of line,"
you would be proud to know that when he raises his voice
it's enough to leave a bruise.
He'll do anything to make you happy.

For his best friend, who is also his roommate, and watched me lie
   on the floor in a fetal position,
closed the door because it wasn't his business,
and listened to my skin split between his knuckles,
congratulations on your baby girl.

To the father at the 7-Eleven who had to teach his son
that a man should never put his hands on a woman,
I'm sorry if your son had more questions than you had answers.
Thank you for asking me twice if I was okay.
You remind me of humanity.
But if you were ready to be a hero, you'd have known I was too
   afraid to say no.

Mr. Officer,
you confirmed that I am a good actress and I must deserve
   this award.

I will remember you if ever I am being too optimistic in believing
    that help is on the way
and he will stop long enough for me to wipe the blood from my
    bottom lip.

Poets who think I don't know how to be vulnerable, that want me
    to unball my fists,
I am protecting myself.
You should've seen what happened when I didn't.

To my father, whose first time being a dad was when I called you
    with the blues
and you had a lump in your throat the size of Texas.
You remember the types of beats you used to make on my
    mother.
Your silence was deafening.
We be a house of blues, daddio.
Baby Girls' got heart.
She's got eyes like your favorite song.

My mother,
who knows me as her golden,
who always blended her smile and strength with blush,
I am embarrassed.
Please touch me up.
Mommy, don't ask for the details.
Do you remember when you didn't want to talk about it?
Can you just hold me
call me baby
make healing like "I love you"?
I need beautiful sounds like that.

To my ex-boyfriend,
whose touches feel like thunder,
whose words bring rain.
I still think about you in my bones
and frontal lobe
when people tell me they love me.

You win.

For anyone who has to come behind him,
I'm sorry it won't be easy.
Can you love me in a way we can both agree on?
Only use words I can recognize and please don't use mine
    against me.
There is a difference.
Pay attention to my body to know which parts are storing pain.
Memorize how many muscles it takes to smile and make sure my
    face isn't missing any.
If ever you make me cry,
be soft enough to make them stop.
Use your hands to couple mine.
Let the only time you raise your voice be to remind God that I am
    a good thing
and you are blessed because of it.

VILLAGE

Where was your village
when they gapped her wide,
left auto-tune residue on her thighs,
called her bitch, and poked her face?

Where was your village
when they drowned out her cries,
dressed her in pop culture, and told her she was just like
    the others;
when they made her drink purple,
leanin' codeine,
sayin' she don't need to educate,
they will jam her even if she's talking about nothing?

Where was your village
when they brought her above ground,
distorted her voice,
called her cute?
Now, that's her only choice.

Well, I am asking you,
like Angelou asked 2Pac,
"When was the last time anyone has told you, that it is
    all for you?"
The sit-ins, the boycotts, the separate but equal.
This is all for you.
There is no limit.
You are doing that to yourself.
God
is on the other side of the wall,
across the bridge,
and over the rainbow.
He is calling the ghetto heaven.
There is nothing wrong with where you come from,
but don't sell out for a generic hip-hop.

He is saying
perfection only comes from the constant act of doing
and we are struggling to make it.
Meeting needs,
drinking Kool-Aid,
but wondering why we're still thirsty.
Conforming, smoothing our edges.
If you are not careful,
you will be round instead of square.

All the while,
the woman who watched her grow is standing there
looking over the city in statue,
still draped in a long dress,
tired of holding a burning burden in her hands.
They have stripped away the veins from her neck, so it looks like
    she's not screaming,
wondering how hip-hop got shackled,
and why the industry is still able to have slave ships on a Red Sea.
R&B is writing,
XO the streets,
XO the hustle,
reminding hip-hop not to forget where she stands in the struggle.
Have a little class.
They won't want it if it's that easy.
Yes,
they
will,
because she is so giving, her oldest baby asked
"Why does it look like the stars are falling down?
Who will stop the cosmos from collapsing into chaos?"
You will.
Even fate picks its hero.
And our village needs you, hero.

Music used to teach us that good was not in everything.
So, if you are sad, it's just because you've stopped reaching.
Stars have daylight hiding places, so at night they shine so hard
they're exhausted,

like language,
like words.
Our words should be firework gun spray.
One day,
your beat will match your words again.
Your past tense will be pleasantly present in your diction.
You will have a heartbeat.
You will have a conscious.
You will be
a hero again.

A HUMAN BEING
LIVES HERE

When my niece asks me how to be a woman,
I want to be able to show my teeth when I smile
and say, "Women love like this..."
but show her the bonesface of misery,
bending knees and yanked hair,
and severely sculptured features.
Say hard work with a hand-me-down back bone,
concealed hand gun,
loaded tongues
hiding nothing but suffering everything.
Forgotten,
like dust buildup behind the TV.
Angular women.
The stretch,
the marks,
9cm long and wide left lonely.
Fittingly enough.
Incomparable.
Accused.
Thick skin.

Building crowns and then giving them up again.
Good cooking, good goods, the leftovers, they look you over.
There's women, and then there's everybody else.
Hurricanes and warm weather.
The beat of old drums.
Rolled up sleeves and blue jeans.
The bow in a bandana.
Bionic collarbones.
Delicate legs, whimsical touch.

This road, this way, is dark allies and too many kissed foreheads.
Red light specials, coupon clipped women.
Remembered for all the wrong reasons.
There's the fight,
combat boots,

the original superheroes.
They gone be mad, let 'em.
We got work to do!
The day of nauseated Americans,
repetitive jokes,
the death of Big Mama.
The day they won't understand your poems.

Be woman.
Something of a warrior,
something of an orator,
operator,
with the biggest appetite, letting you eat first.
Crotch mouth,
crow toes,
eagle wings.
Can't sleep 'cause the brain don't do nothing but think.

A handful of explosives.
Making Kool-Aid, drinking poison.
Gotta prove a point.
I've tried to hide my feelings and use my penis for
    shameless impurity,
but I realize that this is the part of a man I dislike the most.
Without love, we are nothing.

Agamemnon's woman.
But you're just a girl really.
It'll sound different when you're older.
Right now, be mama's baby.
They comin' for you.
I tell her don't grow up too fast.
In this world,
snatchers don't care if you're scared.
There will be men in suits or hoodies eager and inviting
    discomfort,
licking their teeth,
speaking in zig-zag,
making you a sugar glider,
banging on your door trying to get in.

Provoking splinters of silence,
haunting your panties—they won't even remember your name.

When they come, tell them
they won't find no dimes, no cages, or no keys,
but queens and sharks and bullets.
A human being lives here
that be woman and nothing else.
You tell them that your auntie,
Mimi,
nanny,
Bobo,
Aunt Sarah
taught you everything you know.
And you ain't givin' up nothing
not even your ghost.

THE JIG IS UP!

I am not just a large black woman with a heavy throat
or a light-skinned dandelion.
My hair is not nappy.
These kinks do me just fine.
I am not white pages waiting for splattered ink.
I am not young breath or unfamiliar sounds.
I am not jigaboo dances or square fits.
Call me rhombus.
I am not your blues or just any shade of green.
I do not live in shadows, for I was made to be seen.
I am not dry mouth, a safe word, or a morning-after regret.
I am not an empty canvas or drawers where your lover's things
    used to be kept.
I am not a dirty nose, a busted lip, or broken fingernail.
Chipped on all sides but I ain't looking to be yo' diamond.
I am not oversized or fitting in pockets.
I am not heavy handed, a light stepper, or pursed at the lips.
I am not the corner pocket, a pick-up game, or a crap-shoot.
This here be domino.
I am not a sad song, a wild fire, or a little girl playing dress up.

"This is a woman's trip"
and I got my stuff.

I am not new clothes or hand-me-downs.
"I was who I was when I got here."
I am not love notes on bathroom mirrors, your jump-off, your
    backseat groupie.
Matter of fact,
I'll let you know when you can take my picture.
I ain't no shoe rack, no paper stack, no tick or no tock.
This ain't no parking lot, no weak spot, no U-turn, or your excuse.

Sign reads:
ENTER AT YOUR OWN RISK
or
BEWARE OF DOG
CAUSE THE BITCH BITES.

This ain't nothing you can make or break, leave and come back to,
   or use when you choose.

This shit ain't cheap!

I am not a second chance, a rebound, a missed call, an
   afterthought,
a "Baby, Baby please I'm sorry."
I am not fooled by pretty things,
words included.

You can't "beat the pussy up."
That shit ain't even sexy.
This is mine, that's mine, and this and that, too.
This ain't no misrepresentation.
I am not hurt feelings or easily scared.
I am not still standing there when you turn your back.
This ain't no filthy bathroom; my jungle be well groomed.

This ain't no loose booty.

I am not a mistake, the wrong answer, a "Why not?" or just
   because.
I am not neon vacancy, a hum, a doo-whop, or that thing.
I ain't got lemons for your lemonade.
We just eat the cake.

I am not pig-tails, a lolli-pop, or anime.
I am not a fantasy, lipo, or injected.
I know how to walk in heels.
I'm just tired of acting like my feet don't hurt.
Who the hell is Barbie?
This,
this is some grown woman shit.
I cannot,
no,
I will not,
roll over and die for you today.

The jig is up.

THE EXPERIENCE
Story told from the mouth of a Jimi Hendrix guitar

Jimi held the neck of a broom and strummed its bristles when he
     was just a boy,
so I knew he would know how to hold me.
Maple neck,
contour-shaped body,
my mouth pulled sideways.
I am a strat double-cutaway curved open.
Modulated,
I'd scream when it felt right.
My throat,
a burnt rust and bronze ache with the voice of Little Richard.
I learned how to manipulate words by stretching my neck.
I am ebony fret and runaway.
Nobody has ever made me love this hard and easy since.
Sometimes
we would talk for hours making all the right mistakes.
On me, he would freestyle,
breathing from his ears and blowing freak from his palms.
His fingers winking while his thumbs gummed me down.
We gigged, making colors and patterns burst into a purple haze.
I've watched him exaggerate other women with temporary
     feelings.

One time,
I got lost following a loaded shotgun into a mouth another
     country over.
My lover,
sitting too far away from me to reach or call his name.
The military made him heavy without helium.
Pink bullies with brawl-busted knuckles didn't understand
you couldn't have the type of skill my Jimi had and be sane.
At night,
he slept with me to keep us safe.
This
was not crazy.
People

ask what I did with my time when quiet.
I am thinking.
I won't tell them what
or where Jimi was hiding.
We knew how to keep secrets and speak in Neptune.
Ceiling fans would racket over our heads
sending our sounds everywhere.
I'd lay,
a left-handed Hendrix draped across my back,
letting him control me on top.
Plugged in, we were electric.
A furnace lived in my kitchen corner keeping things hot.
Jimi
would sweat and keep his eyes closed when it felt right.

On stage
his hands
would make for continuous wonder flanging,
strong panning,
echoes reverse
phasing rooms and the crowds we fucked.
The "blues is easy to play, but hard to feel."
Until a Woodstock Monday morning legato made the air static
and Jimi made me sound an American blend of war, hope, and
    resentment.
He was the color of fear and patriotism.
The more truth he told,
the more I wailed.
Rockets fell from my mouth.
A shrill lived on the back of my tongue.
We have all experienced doubt in our government.
His heartbeat,
from that day until his death,
has always been,
indescribable.

An old woman now,
rusty,
my frets a bit green,

burnt dimples under the sixth string
with Jimi's DNA all over me,
sits creamy white,
collecting my memories of how I'd follow him everywhere
until I was ancient and well rehearsed.
Not too long or forever ago,
a black man,
flamboyantly dressed,
cool
and always running anew
learned
how to play me
while kissing
the
sky.

STALEMATE

Women make things,
like poetry,
like life,
and love.
They raise Hell,
smile big
oh, and these hands,
these hands be holy and made for healing.
We rock heels and sneakers, sometimes on the same day.
If ever you choose to listen, women are speaking even when their
    mouths aren't.
As a woman,
one of the most powerful parts of our existence is the ability to
    give birth to a child.
Women carry future in the form of forever below their breast,
right under their hearts,
breathe deep and wait until years are ready to happen on the
    outside of them.
The female breed has got to be one of the most important and
    incredible creatures ever created.

So, what do you do with a member of the breed that can't?
At this moment, I'm talking about myself.
At this moment, I'm talking about when doctors say your womb is
    a stalemate
and take these things
and say those things are no good
and leave you with a black hole,
like feeling nothing has always been my purpose.
You never know how bad you want something until you're told you
    can't have it.
I've wondered if this was payback for the abortion
or if God agreed He doesn't want to be a part of any other
    mistakes I make.

Can they look at me and tell?
Do they know I only have half my bag of tricks?

Do I smell like mildew and soggy clothes from the rain?
Are they taunting me by asking if and when I'll have one?
If ever I'm not so polite in my response,
will I be validated for the ebb and flow of anger and pain
that makes waves in my body?
Should I just keep my emotions as basements
and make peace with my eyes
and resist the tears from clawing my face?
It's already hard enough to think about.
Must you be so rude and inconsiderate, too?

How do you tell your lover?
Where will I store his seeds?
Even with the best love-making I've got to give
and the slimmest thickness I've got to grab a hold of

he'll never see the significant mark of his love done right.

Even if love is bigger than fault,
my sheets lined with sorrow will never be a place he'll want to
stay put
and I almost can't blame him.
Tricky how there's a part of me that looks like I used to be able
    to love something here.
How the sparkle in my eyes gives off a glimmer of hope.
The way the Sun is able to find diamonds on my skin
I'll lay dull and colorless in the center of me where we'll both just
    be passing feelings and time
trying to find God or a miracle between my legs.
I don't expect you to want me.

When something is missing,
no one comes looking for me to see if I have it.
Somehow they already know I don't.

"We love because it's the only true adventure."
~Nikki Giovanni

THE FIRST TIME I SAW YOU

The first time I saw you,
I convinced my heart you were the reason it deserved to beat.
You make me want to write love poems on purpose
and it's no accident I don't want you perfect,
because,
if you were,
there'd be no reason to thank you when you change colors for me.

With me,
you don't have to worry about being strong.
I'm willing to love you in pieces.
All I ask is that your heart be whole when you hold me.

The first time I saw you,
I asked my two brown eyes what they loved most about you
when
   they became one
and she said your shadow;
how it gets to love you blind and how that must mean it's a safe
   dare to be yours.
Then she said your hands.
We're all hoping that with all the options you have, you'd rather
   touch me.

Hearts fell from my eyes when you spoke.
Whether you were talking to me or the Sun,
me saying "thank you" in sign language or blowing you a kiss
would
   be one and the same.

When you looked through me like I never existed,
I wrote on my sleeve

"Dear heartache, we've got to stop meeting like this."

My skyline collapsed.
My heart grew fault lines.

The tattoos on my body became scars and I grew stripes.
Is this what concrete feels like?
Is this how a Category 5 picks which home to flood?

I imagine when you're ready,
I'll be wading in the water wasting time,
thinking about you
and waiting on you to see me, too.

HANDS IN POCKETS

He can fit his whole hands in his pockets.
Most times when I've talked to him, this is where they are.
I wonder if he's playing with loose change, writing poems, or if
    this is the way he is most comfortable.

Sometimes, he wears a Members Only jacket and his fingers fit,
but the meat of his thumbs and wrists are exposed.
Maybe, the crook in his elbow making the letter 'c' is when he is
    most open.
I've never seen anyone making x's to his o's, though he told me
one time he was "talking" to someone.
Like what the Hell does that even mean!?
By the way, girls HATE that term, unless
they're the ones you're "talking" too.

I think about his hands when he's long gone and making eye
contact with someone else.
I can't tell if he likes me.
Verbally he has never said so.
Nonverbally, I've convinced myself that he's told me twice,
that he's in love with me,
thinks I'm beautiful,
and can't wait to run his fingers through my hair.
Somehow,
I've also made up in my mind that it's okay if he never says any of
    those things with his lips.
We've both got trust issues, and I'm not sure what I've said to
    him when my mouth wasn't moving.

But we keep it random.

I've written him love notes on my palms in Mehndi with an extra
swirl or dot to mean I'm ready.
We never really are.
Show me your hands and I'll show you mine.

If he's callused,

maybe he's hiding his hurt.
Someone should tell him that every pain he has ever felt is in his
    eyes anyway.
I look like ultraviolets, not disasters.
Is he ashy from dry conversations?
Tired of being the only interesting exclamation point in the room?
Are they frigid and speaking for your enamor?
Nevermind the braille I have for goose bumps.
I stay hot.
I've got plenty of heat.
Young man, you tempt me!

I'd like to be the bristled brush you use to lay down your waves.
Create intimate pictograms of residued stories that have been
    left on our skin.
She hurt you.
He hurt me.
I'm just saying we should write about it and recite healing to
    each other in coffee shops or wine tasting rooms.
"I'd let down my hair, if you asked me to."
Give up all the things that have been a waste of my time and
    replace them with hot breath,
full lips,
and sweet eyes.
Where did the time go?
We've got enough space to last a lifetime.
I'm ready to close the gaps
or at least I think I am.
We've both got shadows in our throats.
Show me your hands and I'll show you mine.

You probably don't like me.
You probably like girls who need saving, carry purses, hate
silence,
and don't give up on their dreams every other day;
girls who always have the right things to say and don't trip over
    their thoughts.

I'm the kind of girl that loves Mondays,

makes herself invisible,
inadequate,
hides inside stripes,
trips over her thoughts,
but can handle the weight of words kept in pockets.

I'd be okay if,
with the next time they're making a showing,
your hands that is,
it'll be to pull me in closer this time.

THE PRETENDER

I keep waiting on you to hurt me,
but you're such a fucking loser, you can't even do that right.

We started off in Eden.
Your hands care for flowers.
You tend to my garden and not one pedal has withered on
  my rose,
but I am not familiar with green thumbs.
Uneven hands can ruin things.
How dare you love me?
How dare you use the "l" word like you don't believe in evil?
In order to believe in one, you had to have been hurt by the other.
Heartache
knows how to swallow everything whole.
Why do you keep trying to save me?
My palms are sweating for a reason.
I am slipping away from this landscape.

I keep loving you in the form of a postcard,
but you keep showing up in my state.
Where is your distance?
Stop
loving me under the earth
through a sparkling sky.
I saw your eyes light up when I said, "I love you."
Honestly,
I am too afraid to really love you.
Honestly,
I am waiting on you to turn grey

to be cold.

Come on.
I know you can do it.

It's strange the memories we keep.

I hate that you're safe.
Every excuse I make, you follow it up with words I used to be
    able to recognize.
I'd be a fool to let you go.
I keep pushing.
You just keep standing there.
You are too strong to love me.
Even when I am weak,
you hold my hand and tell me to try again;
that love never fails.
Inside the word, you are hiding beside me;
said you keep finding me here.
You know that I'm "it", but will not tag me until I'm ready.
Who are you!?
You keep speaking in the Song of Solomon,
but I have been told there is no more good in Solomon
and I know that you will never treat me as if I am a good thing.
So, don't you dare lie to me and tell me that I am a good thing.
I will not fall for your tricks.
I will not love you back.
Protection is my value.
Venus can vouch for that.

Quote:
"A woman who has never avenged herself
has peace on her lips and war in her heart."
This guard comes with purpose.
You are wasting your time trying to tear it apart.
My track record has never chosen an honest person to love me
    consistently.
You say,
never say never.
That's how Jesus got his following.
Okay.

In order not to ruin the surprise,
I will close my eyes
and hold my breath.
Go ahead and hurt me.

I like it better this way.
I like being able to pick you out of a line up.
You say you're different.
I've told you you're all the same.

I keep waiting on you to hurt me,
but you're such a fucking loser you can't even do that right.

NUMBER ONE FAN

When your ex-boyfriend e-mails you and tells you
he's your biggest fan and that he loves you still

drag your mouse to reply.
Change the font and size,
but leave the color of your words the same black and white.
Now is not the time to be fancy or appealing.
Get up.
Fix yourself a bowl of Lucky Charms.
Let them sit.
Turn on the TV.
Make it mute.
Right now, all you need to hear is your thoughts and your
    heartbeat.
Take your cell phone and go through your missed calls.
This should remind you of how many times he wasn't there
    for you
or checking for you
or making sure you were okay
or most of all
how available you always were.
Throw your cell phone in a downward spiral with smashing intent.
Mean it.
Cry.
Hard.
Harder.
Wipe your mascara to the point of eye burn.
Walk to the bathroom assume the position in front of the mirror.
Look at yourself.
Look at yourself real good.
Be clear about who this woman is.
Try to speak.
Try to say something like,
"I love you."
Be clear in what trying sounds like when your lips aren't moving.

Go back to the remains of your cell phone.

Pick up the pieces like you were always left to do.
Hold them
Look at what broken feels like.
Hey, gurl, there's no need to be gentle once broken is done.
Some things will never work the same anyway.
Glitches happen.
Drop those chips again like jacks.
Throw your body onto the floor in a compromising arrangement.
This is for the times he left you there empty.
Say your name,
rigid and nonchalant.
Let it slice through the creases
like blood through chapped lips.
This is for the times you weren't careful and didn't listen to
    yourself.

Sit there.
Sit there.
Sit there.

Hold yourself.

Sit there.

Your tears are stale now to your half moon
and you're crusty to the nasty things he said
and what about everything he did to your heart.
Let's be real:
You're STILL a little salty about it.

Your dog will want to give you a kiss.
Let it.
If you don't have a dog,
get one!
Smile half way like that glass of water you thought you were too
    full to drink.
Think back to the happiest moments you've ever had,
especially the ones you accomplished without him.
Be clear.

Now is not the time to forget how much you matter.

Go back to where your laptop and bowl of cereal sit.
Re-read the message.
Is it worth being soggy?
Love be an uncomfortable thing to hold onto when the texture
   ain't got no grip.
Tears happen for a reason, but why relive these moments?
As much as you want him to you know, he doesn't mean it.

Hit cancel.
Click okay
Log out.
Fans come and go.

DIGESTING LEPIDOPTERA

I wrote poems to my butterfly belly to keep their wings from
   eating me alive.
My shoulders are a giggle box vibration to your copper heart strings.
Rolling clouds.
Paddle wades without the sight of the shore
making me seasick to daydream.
Were your arms calm,
I call them the sky.

My mouth is open.
Humming birds live here
in the back of throats
moving faster than lips can speak.
I am cages of lockjaw.
I thought I was speaking.
I am silently mastering the way my bicuspid aorta valves adore you
in pickle jars
and the bottom glass of Southern lemonade.
I will try more things with you.
Like
Menudo
the Sex Pistols
flannel shirts
a white tee with two fingers and a tongue sticking out with
   fenders for backbones.

My lips can turn red,

I swear.
They be a cacophony of calypso and hip-hop.
You gotta know,
the gap in my teeth be a civil rights movement.

Free thinker,
I am free-thinking without the thought of what it will cost to
   love you
and then scare you away.

This is where beautiful things come to die.

Wild women speak in shaking bush;
green leaves with no limbs.

I know how to love things,
just not always how to keep them.

All the trees have gone.
They took the Sun, too.
If you're not afraid of the dark,
I hide the best ways to love me on the other side of the Moon.

Sometimes I smile.
Sometimes I cry.
I can't remember which one comes first.
You'll have to remind me.
They both have a pulse,
its vernacular is eons.
When you cannot understand it,
that is when you will know what she is saying.

Whirlwind.
A tornado never wakes knowing it'll be a hurricane,
a tunnel,
a disaster.

I am building up to something,
I swear.
. . . .
A butterfly that did not get eaten before
has been at my window for hours
waiting
on the others to come up through my
mouth.
Yellow belly.
Honey,
sticky fingers,
I'm writing sweet things about you with no way out.

VADA & THOMAS J'S
FIRST KISS

When your best friend calls you beautiful,
you wonder why he didn't use gorgeous instead.

We grew up an ashy color of carefree shine.
The only version of the ghetto we knew was to play in God's
    backyard with the duration of Texas heat to beat against
    our backs.
Back
when boys and girls were allowed to be seen together without
    the expectation of them ever holding hands.
Reassuring each other that black is beautiful and that laughter
    was the only thing that mattered.

The summer I got my period my response was much like Vada's
"Get outta here! And don't come back for 5 to 7 days!"
I disappeared inside my hands that year.
I learned the magic of full breasts and how to tape them down.
I wanted my pecks back.
The bee stings made me fill out in other places.
When teased if he and I were an us, we knew people had begun
    to notice that our parts fit.
So, in high school we kept enough distance to fool XY
    chromosomes.
I stopped using duck tape and
I started letting the length of my hair touch the middle of my back.
I told assumptions that I was only loud because I was really
    actually shy!
Later in life,
I will learn the truth is
sometimes I can be really insecure;
that the pigment of my topcoat would make people second-
guess
    how I should be loved.

Ebony will forever mean black.
Forever be misunderstood.

He started taking more showers.
He started wearing name brand clothes, cologne, and a fro.
Other girls wore his letterman jacket.
Freshman year, I learned how to use my silence and my shadow for
    whenever a prettier girl than me was around.
I gave my words bad posture and spoke with my hands closed.
There was nothing ladylike about me.
I used the phrase "I don't care!" so much that it became a curse
    word in my mother's house.
I'd be in danger of losing all my privileges and privacy.

When he was a senior my junior year,
he fell in love with a dandelion and forgot about this Venus
    flytrap of a mouth.
The gentlest thing about being able to catch insects was
    knowing how to digest a vertebrae.
I'd have nothing holding me up whenever his everything was around.

We spent the next 4 years, maybe 5, looking at each other
    through finger-barred jails.
Opening and closing our language like Roman window shades,
we built all kinds of empires during our winters away.
His crumbled first.
I offered the best balled fist I had for her face to restore his smile.
No real friend can stand their best friend hurting, no matter how
    much you hate her guts,
but he had been reading a book that would teach him forgiveness.
Meanwhile,
I learned how to build thicker walls with steel gates, no keys, and
    barbed wire for brains.
He camped out for hours anyway.
This was before Black Friday made it look like a normal thing to do;
that this is just what people had to do to have affordable things.

One night, while changing out my bandages, our lips fell apart on
    top of each other.
Our hands pioneered limited spaces.
We traded energy and touched chronologically.

For the first time, we were a couplet of emotions on accident.
We stopped
before I wanted to,
before I could turn fuchsia,
before I could show him that I wasn't just too many mouths and
   one tongue.

Once we were able to paralyze our passion, words became a
   challenge, too,
but on the inside, I was like "WTF!"
I'm pretty sure that dumb look on his face meant the same thing,
   too.
We were too old to blame this on anyone else.
Both of us silently swore our feelings to couch cushions and let
   TV flicker the brain, our mouths mute.
Click.
He didn't come to my wedding.
My mother saw him that day and said he had on a white suit and
   tears in his eyes.
Click.
He was there for my first real breakup that everyone called a
   divorce.
He built me a bridge and said I can be forever Brooklyn or Baytown,
that he'd be there or here no matter what.
I don't know if that means he's waiting or will come for me.
I
I'm
I'm just hoping he'll call me gorgeous whether we're leaving or
going.

THE SCIENCE OF KISSING

The first time I used my lips in an exchange of words for expression
by pressing their lips against mine,
I kept my eyes open.
I wanted to see what it felt like to touch someone's pyramid,
to mount my mouth onto theirs.

I practiced
on dolls and pillows,
the back of my hands,
mirrors,
and now a person.
A real boy
with humidity, teeth, feelings, and a nose.
Erogenous zones exposed.
We tilted on Earth's axis the way beginners do.
Our heartbeats,
rising and sinking,
making us nervous and unbalanced...
anxious even.
We bounced electric blue current high and natural.
With this boy,
I wouldn't become unraveled or addicted.
I did not bake euphoria or yeast.
The organisms living in our bellies would not lose their appetites,
but that doesn't take away the sweetness of him being my first.

I didn't start using my tongue or notice blood could dilate until I
    got into high school.
Schoolgirl with books and hallways,
the paths I chose.
Larry Lawrence was the first boy to ever make my heart flutter
    and pupils widen.
We sat on our hands if people were around.
Young love in our yester years.
I grew a beauty mark on a right two-headed muscle.
We were never equipped to love weak.
We drove each other apart, like A did Z,

on accident,
but still for a purpose.

Too many times I have kissed with my feelings leading me in and
   without compromise.

As a woman,
I close my eyes every time whether the pyramids are in Egypt or
   outer space.
I use my other senses for figuring compatibility to allow someone
   to feel me soft and magic.
Magnetic moments, I make myself animal and tattoo,
became the taste of love and affection.
When attached to mi baebae,
I am
one part lip-locked everywhere
and another part misbehaving.
Romance balances out the equation.

Chemicals turn our bodies into polyform sculpting clay.
There's an art to everything.
I give my feelings permission and pain a rest when I kiss.
Sometimes I even forget that with lips come hands
and with hands we are able to touch each other while touching
   each other sideways.

The science is also a recipe.
Kiss me and let me know that it's real.
It's all in the findings of making someone fact and alive.

GOING THE DISTANCE

I got my lover from Cali, but he was made in Texas,
where we have bluebonnets, Southern comfort and twang for
   the nexus,
where everything is bigger,
like
his hands,
his lips and feet.
We are too far apart.
Between my heart
and the best I've found yet is 1300mi
12 deserts
2 time zones

and one highway
west.
That road, that way, is a man,
my man,
I get to see every 60 days,
86,000 minutes,
give or take.
The weeks
do not go by faster just because our hearts grow fonder.

We are always in a state of space.

Forever trying to keep the peace and balance.
I know the difference between being bored and lonely;
between love and lust,
a want and a need.
We have learned how to keep the heat while holding mobile
   frequencies to our ears
while our bodies are yearning for each other under the sheets.

Sometimes, he asks silly things like, "Did you miss me?" and
   "How much?"
I say,
"Baby, it's impossible to prove using quantitative data.

However,
the qualitative research shows that I looked at pictures of you
    more than I used my thumbs,
held your name on my tongue more than my own,
and used everyday objects to think of you,
like
the mouse and keyboard – for how many times I wish I were
    touching you,
the floor – I'd lay with you anywhere,
or a spoon – to symbolize the way my body curves into you,
pens
for poems I want to write about you.
This is because I needed another poem to write about you.
Needed something simple and plain.
When loving someone is the sexist thing you got to wear
naked will do.
Wish your touch was one of my tattoos."
A long answer,
a.k.a.
"Boy!
You know I miss you."

So much to where my bones are angry and starving without you
    here beside me.
I keep trying to make my legs long, but that keeps getting me
    nowhere.
I don't care.
I'll move there,
just as long as I can be everywhere your smile is
and get away from this empty room and tears.

I need you here.

This is ridiculous.
This ain't gonna work.
I can't deal or make do.
This is stupid.
Why'd we start this?

But somethings are stronger than doubt.

Like our first kiss after it's been 5,184,000 seconds,
or
how when we're enough,
you're not even willing to let the Moon into the room,
but the stars be our eyes
and we're daylight saving to buy more time.

When touching,
we're back in Texas.
Moving slow,
where warm weather got a breeze and we're a Galileo of
thoughts,
still believing past Galactus.
Holding onto a lot, like love and a planet,
where it's hard,
but worth it
to keep going."

"I know God will not give me anything I can't handle,
I just wish that he didn't trust me so much."

~Mother Theresa

CUPCAKES

Some people smoke weed.
Some people drink Blue Moon or take Tequila shots.
Some people play video games or watch a lot of movies.

I eat
cupcakes.
It's an unhealthy obsession really.
Red Velvet with a sexy white whipped topping find my mouth
    the most.

Cupcakes
are one of the greatest inventions the 1700's ever created.
A cupcake
is a cake to be baked in small cups made for one person.

One person!!!

Don't like to share?
Just need a quick fix?
No one came to your birthday party?
CUPCAKES!

When touched,
an experienced cupcake
knows how to stay smushed together when the paper lets go
but isn't afraid to fall apart inside of your mouth.
The same cupcake knows how to distribute its
flavor and goodness
across a palate.
Knows how to become adhesive to your fingers that can't help
    but be licked.
Delicious cupcakes know how to release endorphins.
Cupcakes are ingenious.

"You can't buy happiness, but you can buy cupcakes.
And that's kind of the same thing."

One time,
I ate a cupcake so good, I woke up in an unfamiliar place.
Cream cheese was everywhere
my hair a mess
I couldn't remember a thing.
Things, were sticky.
My panties were on the floor.
I left them there.
Walked over them and grabbed my keys instead.
I wanted for whoever owned this space to know we happened.
And he or she
was nothing more than a sugar rush
just one of my vices.
A selfish act of instant gratification.

That I can be sweet and leave things sour.

Cupcakes
are a quick fix that doesn't last long.
I should know.
I eat a lot of cupcakes.
I bet I know how to make a stomach hurt
how to make a mouth water
then dry out.
I bet I know what it feels like for someone to get tired of me.
To be something so good and then too much or not enough.
To be crumbs.

I guess the cliché of what they say, is right. You are what you eat.

"Hey cupcake. Who you callin' cupcake?"

LOVE UNDONE

We've been here before.
The door,
me,
him,
threats.
He wants to leave again.
I cannot let him pass.
This too shall pass.
I'll say something to make him stay.

   1: My lips have parted. My tongue is lifted.
     I'll say I love you.
     This time I'll mean it like the first time you heard it.
     Do you hear me?

   2: I'll take your hand, bring it to my chest,
     in the middle of my breast and right in the left of things:
         There is something alive.
         You put this here.
         Boom Boom
         Boom Boom
         We are fading.

   3: I will stare into your eyes,
     recreate the sunset so we can rise together,
     be the first day you saw me.
     Don't see through me this time.
     I can map you a maze
     so where you stand
     here
     is right where you belong.

   4: Your hands are now caressing a cocoon.
     This caterpillar will soon be our butterfly and we will be
       beautiful together.
     God,
     make me pregnant with his responsibility right now.

You did it for Mary,
and Joseph understood.
Please,
I am desperate for more time to make him stay.

5: If you want to go,
   THEN GO.
   I am so sick of being the blame; the fall of Jericho.
   The boulders you throw shatter walls to my glass heart
   and we,
   my heart and I,
   are tired of walking around bloody at our bottom.
   If I am too much woman for you,
   then I release you of your duties.
   You were always too afraid to fight for your country anyway.

6: In life
   we will say things we do not mean.
   We will fight,
   we will scream,
   we will cry.
   We will make love,
   we will make love,
   we will make love.
   We will fight,
   we will scream,
   we will cry.
   We will hang up and call back, because love is on the other end.
      Boom Boom
      Boom Boom
      We are fading.

7: My Love,
   "if I have a faith that can move mountains, but have not love,
      I am nothing."
   I hate to rely so heavily on a book of poems,
   but you'd know none of your lines if it weren't for my pages.

Verse 8. "Love never fails."

9: Do not spend a lifetime trying to replace me.
   Do not punish her because in every way I am,
   she can not be.
   Are you prepared to live without us?

10: We've been here before.   (The door)
    Tears be liquid prayers.   (Me)
    We are embrace.   (Him)
    Sliding down in an asymmetrical shape.
    We are exhausted.   (Threats)

Please stay.
I'm sorry.
I will do better.
Things will be better tomorrow.
Boom Boom
Boom Boom
Boom.

TELL THEM

If they ask how everything came to an end,
tell them that we let love lozenge and dissolve on our tongues,
that we talked a little bit about everything and a lot about
   nothing,
that I spoke Russian and you kept speaking Chinese,
that neither of us were willing to learn English.
We sat on two different sides of the world and kept an ocean
   between us.
That sometimes
the Sahara Desert vacationed in our ears.
We were dry.
Both fire and ice.
After the rain,
we were neither,
just veins, and necks, and tart-tasting wine.
Tell them
that we kept everything inside until our bones were peanut brittle,
until everything hurt,
until we made each other sick.

We were clumsy the way we handicapped these feelings.
Tell them
that we were fast cars,
ruby red and Scorpio
believing we could run on forever;
that we were loop loop looping, but couldn't agree on a rhythm
   or style.
Tell them,
You were Jazz, while I paid the price of hip-hop.
Tell them
that you thought in traps,
while I learned how to bottle it up.
Baby, tell them,
that we were a block of mazes,
that we loved each other numb,
so much so to where our feet wouldn't move,,
that compromise lived in silence or a house without a bathroom.

I am a house without a bathroom, I know.

You
had no heat, but covered furniture well.
Tell them that we stopped praying,
stopped believing in God,
and built temples neither of us could walk into.
That the lights went out and we sat in the dark while everything
    came crashing down around us.

I am a hurricane, I know.

Tell them
that I loved you,
that I love you still,
with everything I got,
but not even my poems are enough,
probably because I chose them over you every time.
A life without balance or priority makes for mismatched clothes.
We didn't always like who we were when naked,
but I could see you anywhere else in the world and still want you;
that I knew how to fuck,
when all you wanted to do was make love,
but neither of our actions made sense;
that the rings came off,
but still fit
and sometimes I put mine on, because it still makes me feel
something.
Tell them
that we learned how to make each other laugh,
but not how to keep the smiles or the Sun,
and never counted the stars or took our time;
that we fought our faults,
gave it everything we had.

Punch drunk,
trying to make chess moves.
We made each other old and bitter,
that I kept a file cabinet of reasons to begrudge you,

that neither one of us could stand being wrong or saying goodbye.

Tell them
we are right for each other just not right now.
Tell them
we're sorry,
we failed,
the way losers do.

The end.

DOUBLE ENTENDRE

The typewriter is a gunshot.
One time for the way I loved you
Two times for the strike in our eyes when we met
An ammunition belt of memories
Eyes dead now
My breath is caught somewhere in my chest
Emotions are wild animals
Tears
A bouquet of sharpened flowers mount the brim of what use to
 be eyelids
I's alone.
My insides a Gemini of polyester fabric
with busy fingers
a mind everywhere
anywhere
but here.
Can't stay
Gotta go
Nowhere
Just
away

We could never figure out how to have roots and wings at the
 same time.

A flashback of love the way we planned it.
Before
Before things went pear shaped
Before Pangaea
We
We were a beautiful and fluid penmanship
The ebb and flow of ink and lines that go on forever

Signing divorce papers is like belittling someone's existence.

I used to know how to write love poems with this pen.
It's true

We happened
Now
the Moon has insomnia
The appetite of a hungry hummingbird losing weight

I am the worst version of myself.

Saying I'm sorry doesn't make bumpy smooth.
Toes keep finding gravel and rocks in their shoes
This is what happens when our mouths become uncupped.
When rights give up reason
Two heads turn wayward
A tongue is now too big to take it all back

And I never thought it would hurt this bad
or that the pain would last for always.
Never thought I could be stolen from you
or that my poems would write us loose without my permission
And I keep thinking I'll write something different,
but all broken hearts scribe the same.

HONEY BADGER

The walls started to pop their own pimples and peel away from
the sheet rock, like bubble gum adhesive.
The knobs stayed in place, but there was nothing on the other
side, but a black hole where psychopaths throw away the bodies.
The carpet
stuck to the bottom of any feet, trying to get out.
Trying to escape,
its curl dried.
It smells of rot and things that cannot be repaired.
The dirt rises and tries to evaporate.
When this doesn't work, arms grow from grain and try to speak
in dust.
The windows plea.
They say things.

Anger does not see clearly.
Everything is black.
A nigger.
The tile in the kitchen becomes green slugs.
I will kill them before they get to the drain.
All the clocks have a Rolodex.
Zero
is flashing until it runs out of breath.
The stairs are trying to lose weight,
to disappear.
There is no corner that my furniture hasn't moved to.
The bathroom is praying with the closet.
Both might as well be my fist.
You forget how hard you can hit when you're trying to hurt
    something.
The pages where I write my poetry have surrendered.
They will probably be there when I get out.
My brain becomes a cuff.
I have started speaking in my 'alien given voice.'
It can be scary trying to figure out what an alternative life form
    is saying
when they're from Sector 7.

No matter the compromise,
I plan to kill you.

The dog has gone belly up.
It's a shame.
I liked that dog.
We should've gotten a fish.
They're easier to get over.
My heart is starting to agree with my head.
They will separate again soon.

Your brain was only beautiful when we were together.
I could have destroyed you years ago.
Something's about to break soon.
Oh.
It's just glass.
It's trying to fly like birds, but anger stripped its wings.
Now, it's just naked.

I was naked for you once.
I used my hips and
tongue and
heart.
You will pay for that.

When angry,
the roof is the first to go.
When I'm done with you, the Sun will be tired.
It will change galaxies.
All the crops will die.

You brought this on yourself.

I tried to warn you.
I tried to wait for you to hold me.
I tried to build you a palace,
buy you things,
take you places,
show you things.

I hope your heart is a shack
with only one room,
no running water,
and no heat.
I hope the wind blows the rest of what you have away.

My throat is a seizure.
Porcupines are what I have for lips,
dark streets and back alleys for eyes.
That smell?
Oh, that's just your flesh on fire.
I made time for you to be tortured.
Anger is yellow on my tongue from all the letters I've licked.
I plan to send you far away.

Now,
you'll say anything to keep a plane from crashing into our backyard.
It's too late.
The whole house is shaking.

Jaws are turning inside out.
You think just because you show your teeth, I owe you another
chance.
We're past that.
I let the laundry stay put, my tears are folded in them.
I promised them I'd be human enough to use them again when
this is all over.
I don't lie like you
or say things in falsetto.
My veins are plunging.
It's so loud you can't even feel my pulse.
A zombie ate my heart.
Blood is everywhere.

I have no choice, but to devour you to stay alive.

"He who teaches, learns a lot."
~Unknown

THE ORIGINAL SUPERHERO

Dear Austin,
I teach your kids how to use condoms,
how to avoid risk and to use a clear "No."
I teach them courage, to ask questions, and how to be careful;
the consequences,
emotional, physical and social.
I teach them how to make healthy decisions
and to wait until they're ready.

I teach your daughters
how to love themselves and how to ration it off,
who's not worthy and why.
I teach them self-esteem,
a little thing called permission,
and how nobody has a right to her unless she says so—
mouth, thighs, heart included.
I teach the power of choice.
How to cross her legs and to stop referring to her best friends
    as 'bitch.'

Your sons
will learn how to be responsible, how to treat women, and how to
    think without consulting their dicks;
that just because she didn't hear you, doesn't make it okay;
that using the word 'faggot' is degrading and has a way of
    making someone disappear.

They both will learn that being gay
is not something you get by being friends with someone who is;
that the word "nigger", "nigga", "nigar" has lit more fires than you
    know how to put out,
will cause more fist fights than you have knuckles,
and right when they thought it was okay,
someone will disappear before the regret comes.

I teach your kids strength and build mind muscle

and, every once in a while, I teach them how to dot an 'i' or
    cross a 't';
how to read cursive, write down walls, see in color and believe
    anything is possible.
I give them money, snacks, and the hugs you forgot they needed.
I teach your kids how to blow their noses;
to say "excuse me", "please", and "thank you;"
to go slow;
to do it right the first time or I'll send them back every time until
    they get it right;
that a false sense of entitlement only guarantees disappointment.
I teach your kids to work hard,
that respect is not an option, but a requirement.
So,
Ms. Ebony, Miss E, or Mrs. Stewart will be the only names I
    respond to.

I tuck my cape into my skinny jeans on my way to work.
I wear sneakers in the brand of Get Anywhere, Anyhow.
Yes, Austin, I do it all for them.

ANONYMOUS BOX QUESTIONS A 6TH GRADE BOYS GROUP ASK THEIR SEX EDUCATION TEACHER

Mz Ebony,
If you don't have a condom, can you use a plastic bag?

No. Plastic bags won't protect you from STDs or prevent pregnancy.

Mz Ebony,
Can a girl get pregnant if I put my Peter in her ear?

No. That was an episode from Family Guy; not real life. Also, in this class, we will only use medically correct terms.

Mz Ebony,
What's another word for balls?

Testicles.

Mz Ebony,
Why do girls scream when they have sex and what if the bed breaks?

Women and men make noises during sex as a pleasurable response, in most cases. This is normal and okay. If the bed is not sturdy, then it could break, but hopefully no one gets hurt.

I am trained to answer these questions,
but sometimes I want to say:

If there is a girl that will allow you to put a plastic bag inside her, this is not the girl for you.

Ejaculating into someone, anyone's ear is gross and confusing, because WHY WOULD YOU WANT TO DO THAT!?!

You could say nuts, tea bags, sac, beans, boys, friends...
but who the hell is Peter!??

And all women don't scream, because not all of us need to. The
question you should be more concerned with is "How will I know if
she's faking or not?"
But none of the above has to do with the bed breaking!

But then there are questions put into the box with Tim's name
attached as true as the Sun admits it's a star, with print as small
    as the signature of a gnat.
Evenly folded to show me how careful I have to be in answering
his questions:

Mz Ebony,
Why does liking the color pink make me gay?
And if I am is it bad?

And I immediately wanted to show him how to be camouflaged;
how to give up his shadow and become a closet;
that they have picket signs and slanderous tongues shaped like
    swords of malice made for cutting;
that we all have a certain type of prejudiced bully inside us.
You, boy, must not believe in being outcast
And that blue,
blue is more fitting for the sinking emotions you might feel
or to show the life span of your bruises that haven't quite healed,
yet,
or the color of your iris before a piece of you turned grey.

Tim,
with all 206 bones, 17 of them reaching for me in his eyes,
looks at me the way he does hope and like
the ability to love outside of himself.
Tim is waiting for an answer.

SO, I say,
You can be a pink Spider-Man if you want to,
a bow tie,
a cupcake with pink insides,
just as long as you're a heartbeat.
Preference and colors are attached to emotions, so you should

do what feels good.
You must be willing to be brave enough to be the only one who
    knows you're afraid.
Bad
is hiding inside yourself.
Bad
is someone judging you by what they don't understand or in
    which direction your heart goes,
when love is supposed to be a good thing that you shouldn't have
    to control or use a cookie cutter to recreate;
that love
can be a person, place, thing, or any action you can wrap around
    that special person that makes your heart explode when they
    walk into a room.

There is no skull and crossbones over your heart.
You are a good thing that someone will be dying to get next to.

And Tim says,

Mz Ebony,
Everybody knows that Spider-Man would rather be purple.

DARES

A dare is a verb that behaves like an auxiliary verb, such as CAN
   or MAY,
and is sometimes a main verb, such as WANT or TRY,
to challenge someone to do something, move something, be
   something more.
Example:
   I dare you to have the courage
   required for living.
I dare you
to ask for what you need and expect it to happen the way love
   owes you nothing
but keeps reoccurring.
I am daring you to be bold
to no longer be into self-hatred.
That time has passed.
This heart has healed.
I dare you to use the power you already have
to be worthy
to be more than
because less than doesn't live here anymore.

I have a hard time seeing you or wondering why you exist
if every time push comes to shove
you fall or crumple
run and hide.
Growth is supposed to be uncomfortable.
Dr. Seuss says
   "You'll miss the best things if
   you keep your eyes shut!"
So, I'm taking it up a notch:
I double-dare you to have the guts of your favorite superhero
(Storm, Wonder Woman, Katanna).
I double-dog-dare you to be different
to change where the feelings happen in your body.
Sadness
should be in the feet
because it means you have to keep going.

You're this close to having an impact.

Take these words and dodge bullets.
This is your proof.
May your "words bring worlds" and your heart say fight.

I triple-dog-dare you.

RED & PURPLE SKITTLES

There will be Skittles and short cries.
When life exits the body,
there will be silence.
A village will mourn.
A father will forget how to breathe and walk like men do.
A mother's tongue will turn to sand and mango sticky rice.
Palm trees will lean toward salt water.
A little boy will be scared to enjoy the day unarmed.
He will make his fingers tight.
Someone has stolen his adventure.
Another mother, up the street, will give extra hugs to men that
barely reach her knees.
Her hands will stop at patty-cake.
A girl who makes doodles to the boy she crushes on will not know
    which box to check.
The last time she chose "yes," he never got to see her reply.
A teacher
will teach a ghost in row 3, 5th seat from the back, how to
    slow down.
He pauses
and leaves an indention on her heart.
He was her favorite.
The sky will be empty.
Particles will forget how to bounce and the Sun will fail the
    color blue.
The ocean will lose a ripple and remind grandpa this is not where
you go to skip rocks if you want a reply,
but at night we will speak to the stars,
looking for God or a reason why.
There will only be static.

When children and life go back to habit,
a black woman with a pregnant belly will feel guilty.
She knows this world will remind baby that there is no such thing
    as being innocent.
This elephant she carries is a community.
Someone will replay the tape and sit stoic, unclenched and shuffling.

Her throat will think of the name
Trayvon,
Troy Davis, or
Lamar Smith.
She will choose none of these.
Somehow,
her baby has a purpose and a chance that the others didnot.

My people are bloated apologies with weight 100× its bullet.
Our walks have grown longer and more concentrated.
Skittles,
especially the red and purple ones,
will taste differently.
It'll feel like eating Uluru.
The taste will be lost and fit for dark caves or other places we
try
    to show our hands.
My people will learn that you speak in chops and helicopter
views,
    rocky roads, and self-defense.
You make us believers and Southern tales daily.

When the papers find another reason to rust at the edges
and the news headlines another doctrine,
we will remember where we keep our plastic baggies with more
    tears, exhausted faces, and our riot bubbling spirits.
There is no peace here.

"Nothing is wrong. Everything is an experience"

60 SECONDS

A lot could happen in 60 seconds.
You could
  wash your hands.
  miss the bus.
  make a peanut butter and jelly sandwich.
  take a shot or 2 or 3 or 4.
Or
  send a text message.
  get in a car crash.
  kiss the girl of your dreams.
  count the number of black kids in a Harry Potter film.
  You could lose.
  You could lose bad.
Or
  you could have sex. Maybe not good sex, but, for minute men's
    sake, we'll call it a quickie!
  say your ABCs backwards.
You could
  sit.
  hold your father's hand on his death bed.
  watch him take his last breath.
  say I love you.
  replay his smile
  how loud he could fart.
  how hard his hands were matched.
  how hard he worked
  and how them being soft right now just doesn't feel right.
You could
  hold your breath.
  and try.
  and stop breathing, too.
Or you could
  think of 100 questions you didn't get the chance to ask like
    what's something you always wanted?
And he could say,
  "More time."

BLINKS

The thing about time
is that we have so much of it and then again we don't.

Time is effortless and unapologetic,
never worries about going too fast or too slow.
Time knows there's a time for that.
Time has guts,
like guns being drawn in the Wild Wild West with a man who has
    come to be your enemy,
but looks just like you from afar.
I've pulled the trigger too many times and killed myself for not
    pulling the trigger quick enough.
Blink.
I forgot to tell that one person that one thing about that one
    time they said that one word that put everything into
    perspective.
Blink.
Now she's gone.
Spent too much time standing and pledging to lies in line.
We forget how to pray for peace, because we keep getting ready
    for war.
We didn't even get to see who hit who first.
Blink.
Now, it's all a blur.

My daddy says, If they put they hands on you...
and without even finishing the sentence, we all knew how to
    protect ourselves with our thoughts.
Who cares if I never get no bigger than a fist?
I hit just as hard in Houston as I would in Brooklyn,
but,
this time,
I want you to believe me without me having to show you.

Blink.
I keep looking at fig trees wondering what I've learned,
with all this time,

about being satisfied,
but when you grow up in a small town you know how to find
    laughter in the dirt.
Do something different.
This time,
let's fight about how much we love each other and use words
    like, 'my little gummy bear' at the end of it.
Let's fight about which came first: Voltron or Transformers,
and I can love you anyway, even if you give the wrong answer.
(It's Transformers.)
Let's fight about which parts of my body love you the most and
    the only way to solve it
is for you to touch me.

Blink.
I want to be able to tell my grandchildren stories that start with,
"This one time, at band camp..."
Ray Neal pressed his lips against mine and kissed me the way he
    would his tuba and just as hard.
For a minute or two, I could use that memory to forget about all
    the beautiful moments I've had that turned to scabs.
Gotta stop picking at it.
You gotta stop using alcohol to solve your problems, just
    because you're used to the burn.
I read somewhere that the body knows how to heal itself.
I'm wondering if I've given my heart enough time to learn.

Blink.
Let's take our time like God does,
the way koalas do.
Do you go so fast, because you're afraid of slowing down,
of losing your place,
of people questioning if you're telling the truth?
Here's a clue:
this time, go slow enough for people to believe you and your stories.
Maybe this time you should just mean what you say.
You don't want to waste your time
telling and believing lies when
all you have is a blink.

CURRY ⟩

When you cut yourself while chopping green and red peppers,
do you wait for the smell to move downwind?
For the blood to spread like Marilyn Monroe's lips?
Did you part your own and put sting to bud and wonder why so
    many things don't have flavor?
This way you know what emotions don't taste right.
Loving yourself can be an acquired taste.
Are you the kind of person who needs pain to remind you that
    death is real?
Have you existed past your mistakes?
Seems like there's enough moments you've lived in life where this
    has happened enough times for you to know better.

When you rush water to rinse your wound, do you watch your
ancestors forget how to swim?
This moment is vital.
This moment means you'll spend the rest of your life trying to
    remember how to save yourself.
I've misplaced my manual.
Bet it's in the junk drawer with all the other things I'm not
    making use of, like keys.
Bet one of them opens a piece of my mind that will explain why
    I'm not doing it right.
Does this mean I'm too lazy to solve my own problems?
Got questions that I don't really want the answers to.
If only I knew how to stop this blood!
But something somewhere in my body doesn't do good at
    getting numb,
or giving up,
or knowing when to just let go.

Have you decided which came first:
the way hurt feels when it happens or the way it looks?
Severed,
like the clitoris of hip-hop,
"wet like I get sometimes,"
open,

wide.

You know,

the way women always find a way to compromise themselves and
    smear lies until it feels good enough to be the truth.

Is there a Band-Aid big enough to cover all of this and that?

When throbbing is asleep, do you still ache?

Is it so deep that crimson blooms outside of its given space?

You have no idea how wounds heal.

Maybe because you don't read enough books or get rid of
    outgrown shoes,

but those

those are my favorite.

"Bag lady."

Do you need another Band-Aid?

Or tissue?

Or glass of wine?

And, like that Maxwell song, "This Woman's Worth," you're still
    trying to figure out what you're worth.

Yeah, that song gets you every time.

Jazz ain't no better.

Did you forget how to snap your fingers, sway your hips, or pop
    that gum?

Do you pick at your scabs?

Is this how you teach yourself a lesson?

Do your scars make for incredible stories when you're sipping
    dirty martinis with your girlfriends

and laughing like Ain't life funny(but it's not)

with your heads back and your mouths wide?

Can your laugh be mistaken for a cry?

I know mine can.

Do you hold your stomach because this is where you keep your
    tears?

Can you love yourself?

Can you love yourself?

Can you love yourself?

Fall in love with yourself.

And suddenly,
that was the problem all along.
It's the only way to make the blood stop
and that hollow you wear about your brow
can be worn like a bracelet or bangles.
Call that notches,
or did you just learn how to let go of your own throat?
Call that forgiveness.
Call this healing.
Eat it with roti.

HOW TO MAKE POETRY

inspired by Aja Monet

I know that church is made of praise and hand claps,
   that God lives in goose bumps,
   that a sinner is in everyone.
I know
   that laughter starts in the heart,
   travels to the belly,
   and comes out the mouth.
I know that cooking should be made with love and healing,
   that I must first wash my hands,
   that forgiveness happens once the sting is gone and you have
   an encouraging scab.
I know that a smile can change the quality of my face,
   that my lips can be found in any ghetto you choose.
I know
   that saying what you mean and meaning what you say takes
   practice.
So does making good choices and making Kool-Aid.
I know that mothers learn how to hold their children while they're
   in the womb and take up for them for all the right reasons.
I know how to play outside and how to let the Sun live on my skin.
I know how to treat Earth no matter how much I've cried;
   how to give to people I barely know or maybe not even at all.
I know that being a woman sometimes means being selfless.
My grandmother taught me this.

I know that dancing takes more than rhythm.
I know
   words can cause war.
I am learning how to be careful.
I know being quiet is a skill married to confidence.
I know how to use a stove and how to keep a kitchen clean.
I know that humming is an art made from the things I've
touched;
   that graffiti is what happens when I'm trying to sort things out.
I know that love doesn't change, people do;
   that purpose can be found in fear and facts;

and bravery is a belief.
I believe in being strong.
I know how to make people feel welcome,
  how to give my last,
  how to keep a lover coming back;
that the gap in my teeth represents the division of my ancestors
that never met;
  that men in Paris think I'm sexy;
  that men on the East Side think I'm sexy;
  that men in New York think I'm sexy.
  I know men.
I know that sex is not a remedy for loneliness;
  that touching myself is not bad,
  the body is a memory;
that I write to calm the shadows and to keep from swallowing my
  demons.

I know right from wrong by living and putting shoes on the wrong
feet,
  from glasshouses where I throw my stones.
I know how to lose things.
I know I will see them again.
I know that my mother stayed for her family,
  but left for herself
  to show her children
  that's not how a man should treat a woman.
I know I deserve me, too,
and I know I deserved a mother.
I know that men can throw farther than women,
but women know how to feel things.
Both are needed to make the world go round.
I know
  how to make a fist and a heart with my hands.
I know that fighting doesn't make me mean,
  but means I give a damn.
I know how to use curse words,
  how to water things down,
  and how to save face.

I know that family is home,
is forever.

I know how to make poetry, like this.
How to make love, like this.
My grandmother taught me this,
I know.

NOTE TO SELF

Dear Universe,
I'm still standing here.
I'm still loving here, in this body, with this heart.
Peace be,
love be,
forgiveness be,
and I dare you to try and stop me.
I love you, because you're worth it,
because you're a good thing,
because I can.
There.
Take that!
Note to self: Take chances, on purpose.

When the voices turn on you,
when you're soggy and soiled,
when something is telling you "you can't do it,"
your insecurities are showing.
Stop it!
You have permission to fight back.
You have permission to love you first.
Where you gone get another one?
those eyes,
these hands,
that laugh match the way you walk.
Who told you you had time to be sad?
Nevermind those tears.
Them, like all the others, don't stand a chance.
Wipe them,
like this.
Let them see you,
like that.
This is me loving hard with both hands.

Note to self: Forgive yourself, heart included.

Sometimes you're in your own way.

Move,
like time,
like worry.
Sprinkle courage.
Pour confidence.
Mix.
   Here you go,
   Be brave.
Now, believe it.
Go the distance.
Move from hoping
   to making it happen.
Change your mind.
Go with your first mind.
Love.
Even when you don't want to,
even when they don't deserve it.
When I love,
I love on purpose.
What's love got to do with it?
Everything!
Your life is depending on it.

Make rhythm.
My clarity.
Make lists.
It only takes five fingers to push on:
   1. Be positive
   2. Stay positive
   3. Love
   4. Pray
   5. Grind on

Get out of your own head.
Breathe.
Pay attention.
Be slow to speak.
Listen.

Note to self and keep reminding yourself: Don't attract negative
   thoughts or people. Their egos don't belong here.

Dear Depression,
   You can leave now.
I am aware of the energy I bring into a room.
I gotta French kiss fear with this mouth.
   Now is a good time to say I was here.
That's permanent,
like hugging yourself.
Hug yourself.
Mmmm that feels good.
Mmm-Mmmm nobody does it better.

Misplacing yourself is equivalent to losing your mind.
Take that back.
Forget where you put people and things that don't love you back.
Trust yourself.
Believe in self.
Take what you need,
but give everything
and you might not have much,
but fight for the little bit you have.
When a poem finds you, you have no choice but to believe in God.
This thing is bigger than you.
I choose me.
I choose me.
I choose to live life to the fullest.

Quote: "I found God in myself and I loved her, I loved her fiercely."

And when I love,
the way I love,
I love on purpose.
And you
can't stop me.

12.21.12

If the world ends tomorrow
I'll be able to say I knew love.
Its touch, the way it smells and tastes, the way it looks dark
  brown with dimples;
That I made love once and it didn't hurt
That it held me afterwards and called me gorgeous
That it felt like what I thought my first time was going to feel like
That it made me a believer and forgiver with breath
That I loved hard as minerals, all kinds, on different days
That my father will always be one of my reasons or excuses.

If the world ends tomorrow,
I didn't like Bar-B-Que, watermelon, chicken, having a period,
or college. I also didn't care what other people thought about
this. I could make some bomb-ass Kool-Aid, write poems that
understood you, and give hugs that made people forget about
all of the things that made me "weird." I loved to travel and
dream in different cities. Poetry is responsible for most of this.
I wrote the truth. It was all I had. I am writing still somewhere
atop a comet. In most cases, this is the way I loved on purpose.
I listened to so much music my brain was an iPod before iPods
existed. I got this from my dad. I danced. Well. And could move
my hips into a tornado.

I probably got this from my dad, too. Both of our anger was a
hurricane. Neither of us wanted people to know or remember us
that way. So my eyes were my mothers. My eyes were galaxies
and the ascension of hope.

If the world ends tomorrow,
You should know that I cursed. A lot. That it made me feel good
and almost every time I meant to do it, but knew when not to.
I had manners. That I read a lot of books, but never enough. I
knew too many words to ever be handicapped, broke, or dumb.
That my hair and my strength were one strand. I had a lot of
them. I tried to live a daredevil life in the state of mind of a
storm. I had friends that I'd take to the back alley with me to

whoop some ass or have a conversation of logic. They are the only ones who understood they'd have to forgive me often. They know who they were.

If the world ends tomorrow,
I didn't always like being called black, but loved the color. America was confusing. It probably still is. I ate cupcakes to make up for the bad days, and wore sneakers so I'd be comfortable and flyy.

If the world ends tomorrow,
Whether astrology was bull corn or not, what they had to say about Scorpios has always been true. I refused to have a favorite. I hated nothing and did my best to remove it from my mouth and figurative mind. I learned that presence has nothing to do with speaking. I was a good teacher who continued to learn about herself through her students. The children that lost their lives during the Sandy Hook Elementary School shooting didn't haunt me to hurt me, nor was it on purpose.

If the world ends tomorrow,
The most important thing you needed to know is that women raised me. They made me all black girl Barbie and Gully at the same time. They didn't regret any of it. I had a great childhood, balled fists, scrapes, and bruises. My mother taught me how to smile and to be slim thick. My sister was the first person to ever make me laugh. I loved to make people laugh. My brother was the first man I ever believed in. My nephew Zachary was the last man-child I ever believed in.

If the world ends tomorrow,
Having OCD is one of the hardest things I've ever done repeatedly right and wrong at the same time. That's why God gave me the choice of pizza and my mother's cooking. I believe there's a God in all of us. I believe fear causes us not to believe in anything at all.

I believe that the Universe did not let me fail.

Love always,
Ebony Stewart

P.S. Zombies cannot climb trees and katanas should be kept sharp.

EBONY STEWART

www.thegulleyprincess.com

With lips from any ghetto you choose and words spoken to save her own life, this Gully Princess by the name of Ebony Stewart, is the only adult female Three Time Slam Champion (2007, 2009, 2011) in Austin, TX. She has shared stages with Amiri Baraka, is currently the top ranked female poet in Texas, nominated one of Austin's "MUST SEE", was one of the leading members of the Austin Neo-Soul slam team in 2010, ranking 4th in the Nation, and co-coached the Neo-Soul slam team, taking them all the way to first place in Group Piece Finals, in 2012. Poetry is where Ebony Stewart goes to make things right.

Currently, Ebony Stewart is probably eating a cupcake, reading a comic book, or searching for some fresh sneakers. That is, if she's not teaching Sex Education to sixth and seventh graders.

ACKNOWLEDGEMENTS

"If I have seen further it is by standing on the shoulders of giants."
~Issac Newton

The thing about standing on the shoulders of giants is some-
times you don't even know you're doing it until it's done. So this is
for the shoulders I have stood on and those shoulders to come.

The Universe has its own set of shoulders that will not let me fail.

To my mother, the biggest giant I know. The first poem I ever
met and reason I curve lines, laugh lines, and love long. She was
made for me so I write poems for her.

To Austin Neo-Soul, thank you for finding me, for giving me my
own room in the house that Herman & June built. Thank you for
allowing me to be a beautiful Vriesea flame.

The poetry community that I have found in you all that now ex-
tends across the nation is incredible. I am left speechless every
time I think about it.

To every poet in the state of Texas whether a visitor or native, I
say, TELL THEM... ALL OF THE THINGS!

Funky Mike Whalen, you are one of the most attentively, pure,
and good people I have ever met. Not enough people know of
your skill and talent. I am honored to be one of your top five.

Brian Francis, Brently, LaLove Robinson, Shay, Korim, Danny
Strack and Zai thank you for being a wrist and a fist of unstoppable
truth-telling. Swear I became "unfuckwitable" through your
poems and energy.

Dear Ariana & the whole 2012 They Speak Under 21 Slam Team,
what an incredible group of constellations. I am sucking all the
youth from your heads as you read this. You make me better...
next stop, the Moon.

To the Xenogia Spoken Word Collective, only ninjas and good music know what it means to feel the way I do for you.

Jomar Valentin my 300 year-old boy, I love you and your words, the cat in your poetry and the jeans your booty fits in. Patti Rice can borrow my clothes anytime.

Amir Safi, you get me and that's enough.

Lacey Roop we're trouble, combat boots, and flyy to death together.

Kevin Burke your tattoos are cool, your poetry is better. If I were ever to be a white man... okay, I'd be Thor, but you're totally punk rock and that's still love.

To my family & friends that made me, put up with me and the way I life love flaws and all, with closed fists, I am learning and doing more to make you proud. Thank you.

There is a God in my pen. I am thankful for the poems that choose me.

Timber Mouse thanks for believing in me, my words, and ability. Thank you for line breaks and formatting. For a lack of better words and it still being the truth, I am so blessed to have you all in my corner. Thank you for making my darkness good and my black a twilight.

To the eyes that are reading this right now, thank you is an understatement. Thank you for using your fingers to hug my pages. Please know that you make me worth it and keep me vulnerable. I hope to become one of your favorites or at least someone that you really really like.

CPSIA information can be obtained
at www.ICGtesting.com
Printed in the USA
LVHW110149250320
651137LV00001B/39